KinderMath Printables

Easy Peasy

All-in-One
Homeschool

Lessons 6-28

0   1

2   3

4   5

6   7

8   9

Lessons 6-22

Use this page for practice writing each number from lessons 6, 11, 17, 21, and 22.

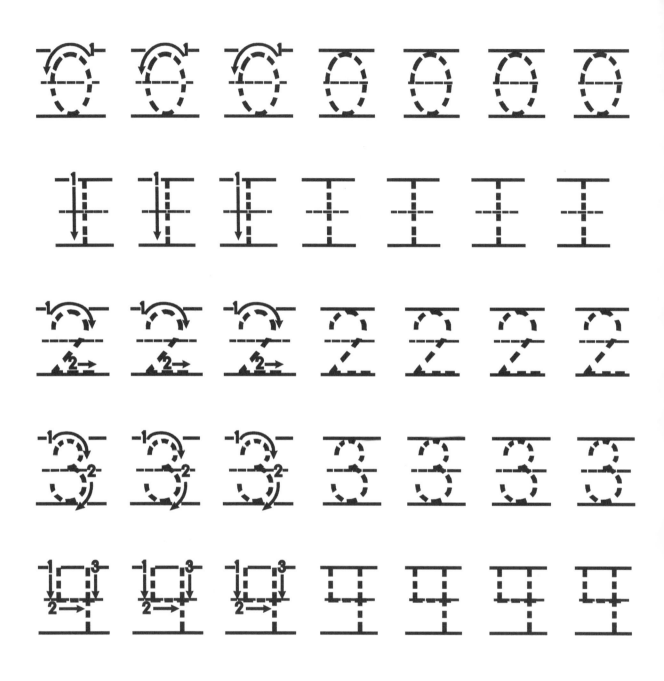

Lessons 23-28

Use this page for practice writing each number from lessons 23, 25, 26, 27, and 28.

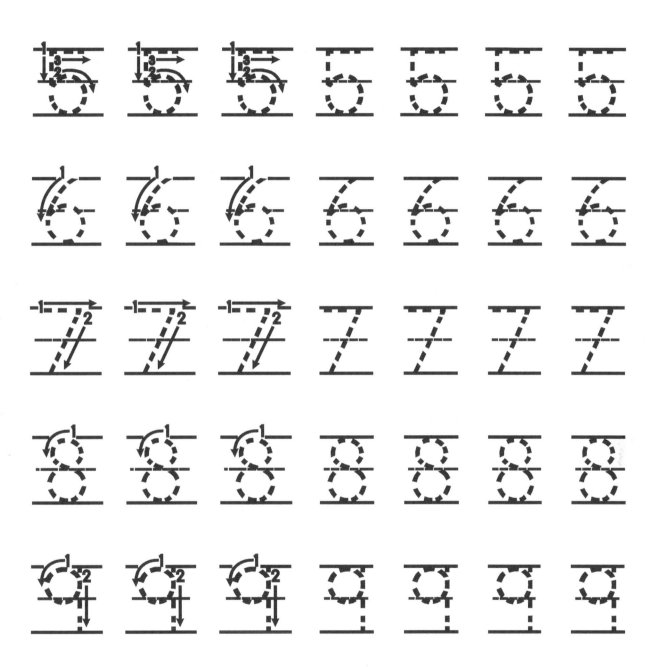

Help the Squirrel Find the Acorn – Lesson 58

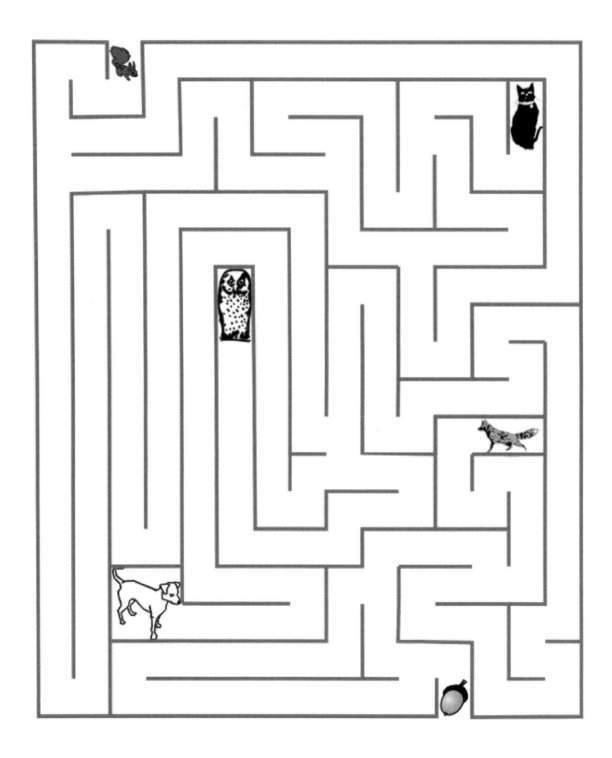

Writing Equations and Adding 1 – Lesson 96

Write 5 + 0 = 5.   Write 3 + 1 = 4.

_____ + _____ = _____   _____ + _____ = _____

4 + 0 =   5 + 1 =

7 + 0 =   8 + 1 =

1 + 0 =   6 + 1 =

Lesson 106

_____ + _____ = _____   _____ + _____ = _____

Lesson 120

_____ + _____ = _____   _____ + _____ = _____

Writing and Modeling Equations – Lesson 97

Write 3 + 1= 4.   Write 1 + 3 = 4.

_____ + _____ = _____   _____ + _____ = _____

Draw a picture that shows the equations above. Show three of something and show one more. There should be four all together.

Writing Equations – Lesson 106

Write 2 + 3 = 5.   Write 3 + 2 = 5.

_____ + _____ = _____   _____ + _____ = _____

Writing Equations – Lesson 120

_____ + _____ = _____   _____ + _____ = _____

Counting On – Lesson 121

Practice counting on. When we're trying to figure out addition problems we count on. Go around the board adding on 1, then 2, then 3. Color in each spot you land on. Start is 0. The first thing you'll do is add 1. So, you will color in 1. Then you will add 2. So, you will count 1-2 and land on 3 and color in the number 3 space. You can keep track of what you are adding by crossing off the numbers at the bottom of the page.

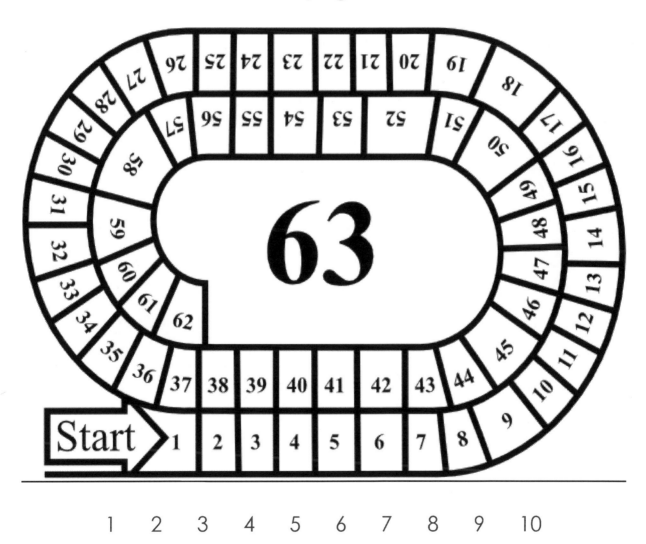

1   2   3   4   5   6   7   8   9   10

How many more do you need to add on to make it to 63?

answers: 1, 3, (count on 3) 6, (count on 4) 10, (count on 5) 15, 21, 28, 36, 45, 55 (8 more to 63)

Adding on Number Lines – Lesson 122

Below is a number line. It can help you add. Put your finger on 2. Jump three numbers to the right. That adds three. What number are you on now? Right! It's 5. 2 and 3 more is 5. **2 + 3 = 5.**

2 + 3 = 5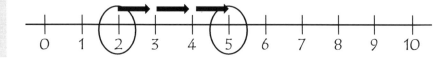

Use the number line to add. Write the answer in the box.

2 + 4 = ☐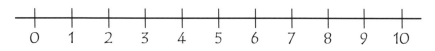

3 + 5 = ☐

1 + 7 = ☐

9 + 0 = ☐

6 + 3 = ☐

8 + 2 = ☐

3 + 6 = ☐

7 + 1 = ☐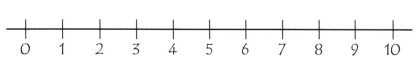

Counting to Add – Lesson 123

Count the objects to add. Write the answer in the box.

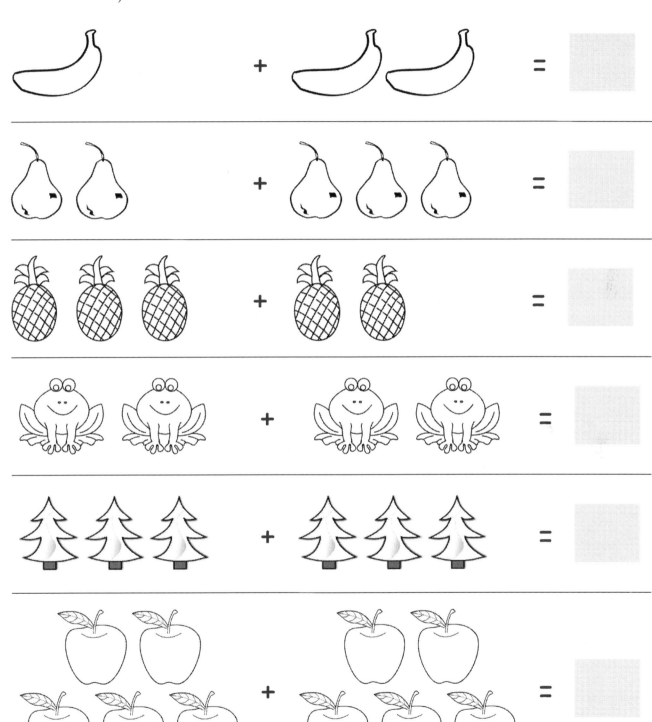

Counting to Add – Lesson 124

Count the objects to add. Solve each problem and read it out loud.

2
+ 2
4 Two plus two equals four.

2
+ 3

3
+ 2

3
+ 3

2
+ 4

4
+ 2

3
+ 4

4
+ 3

4
+ 4

Practice adding 0 and 1. Read out loud each problem.

3	1	2	1	0	1	1	4
+ 0	+ 4	+ 0	+ 0	+ 4	+ 3	+ 2	+ 1

Counting to Add – Lesson 125

Complete each addition sentence to make 5. Count each type of bug and write in the number. In every line there are five bugs all together.

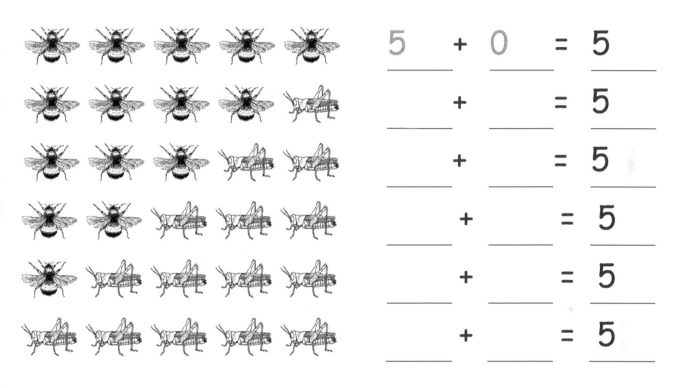

5 + 0 = 5

____ + ____ = 5

____ + ____ = 5

____ + ____ = 5

____ + ____ = 5

____ + ____ = 5

Subtract One and Zero – Lesson 131

3 – 0 =   7 – 1 =

6 – 1 =   5 – 0 =

Counting to Subtract – Lesson 136

When you subtract, you take away some objects from a group. **5 − 3 = 2** means "you take away 3 objects from a group of 5 objects and 2 objects remain." Draw **X** over the objects to take away. How many objects remain?

$5 \quad -1 \quad = \quad \boxed{4}$

$5 \quad -2 \quad = \quad \boxed{}$

$5 \quad -3 \quad = \quad \boxed{}$

$5 \quad -4 \quad = \quad \boxed{}$

$5 \quad -5 \quad = \quad \boxed{}$

$5 \quad -0 \quad = \quad \boxed{}$

Subtracting 1 on a Number Line – Lesson 137

You can use a number line to subtract. Put your finger on 10. Jump one number to the left. That's subtracting one. Write the answer. Jump one more. Write the answer. Keep doing the same until you get to 0.

10 – 1 = 9

9 – 1 = 8

8 – 1 =

7 – 1 =

6 – 1 =

1 – 1 =

2 – 1 =

3 – 1 =

4 – 1 =

5 – 1 =

Counting to Subtract – Lesson 142

Draw X over the objects to subtract. Count the remaining objects.

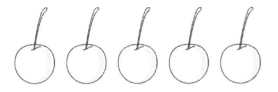   

5   - 1   =   4   5   - 2   =   ____

4   - 1   =   ____   4   - 2   =   ____

3   - 1   =   ____   3   - 2   =   ____

2   - 1   =   ____   2   - 2   =   ____

Color by Number – Lesson 144

1 = Black   2 = Brown   3 = Pink   4 = Green   5 = Blue   6 = Yellow

Color the Shapes – Lesson 145

Rectangles = Orange   Triangles = Red   Ovals = Brown
Diamonds = Green   Circles = Blue   Squares = Yellow

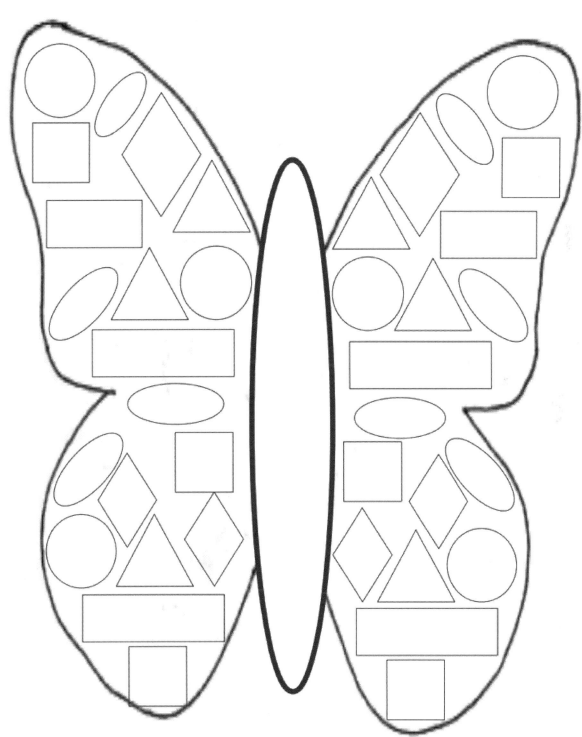

Lessons 146-165

Write: 1, 2, 3, 4, 5

_____

Write: 6, 7, 8, 9, 10

_____

Write: 11, 12, 13, 14, 15

_____

Write: 16, 17, 18, 19, 20

_____

Write: 21, 22, 23, 24, 25

_____

Write: 26, 27, 28, 29, 30

_____

Write: 31, 32, 33, 34, 35

_____

Write: 36, 37, 38, 39, 40

_____

Write: 41, 42, 43, 44, 45

_____

Write: 46, 47, 48, 49, 50

_____

Write: 51, 52, 53, 54, 55

_____

Write: 56, 57, 58, 59, 60

_____

Write: 61, 62, 63, 64, 65

_____

Write: 66, 67, 68, 69, 70

_____

Write: 71, 72, 73, 74, 75

_____

Write: 76, 77, 78, 79, 80

_____

Write: 81, 82, 83, 84, 85

_____

Write: 86, 87, 88, 89, 90

_____

Write: 91, 92, 93, 94, 95

_____

Write: 96, 97, 98, 99, 100

_____

Fill in the Numbers – Lesson 167

Count to 100 and fill in the missing numbers.

1	2		4	5	6	7		9	10
11		13	14	15		17	18	19	20
21	22	23		25	26	27	28		30
31	32	33	34	35	36	37	38	39	
41	42	43	44		46	47	48	49	50
	52	53	54	55	56		58	59	60
61	62		64	65	66	67	68	69	70
71		73	74	75		77	78	79	80
81	82		84	85	86	87	88		90
	92	93		95	96	97		99	100

Counting to Subtract – Lesson 172

Draw **X** over the objects to subtract. Count the remaining objects.

5 - 1 = _____

5 - 3 = _____

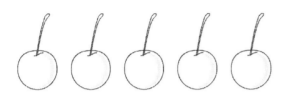

5 - 4 = _____

5 - 2 = _____

4 - 4 = _____

4 - 2 = _____

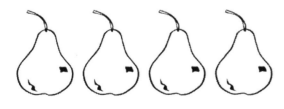

4 - 1 = _____

4 - 3 = _____

Counting to Subtract – Lesson 175

Draw **X** over the objects to subtract. Read aloud the problem and answer.

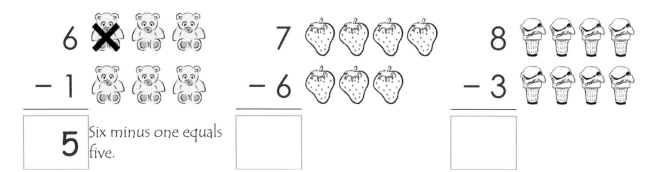

6 − 1 = 5   Six minus one equals five.

7 − 6 =

8 − 3 =

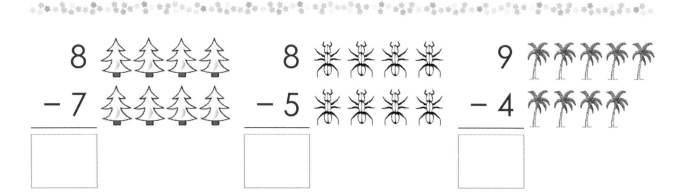

8 − 7 =

8 − 5 =

9 − 4 =

9 − 8 =

9 − 5 =

10 − 9 =

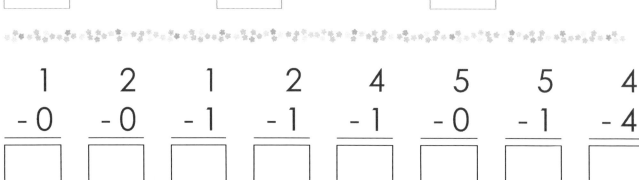

1	2	1	2	4	5	5	4
− 0	− 0	− 1	− 1	− 1	− 0	− 1	− 4

*This page is for cutting. The back is intentionally left blank.

19	20	nineteen

twenty	I	II

III	IV	V

*This page is for cutting. The back is intentionally left blank.

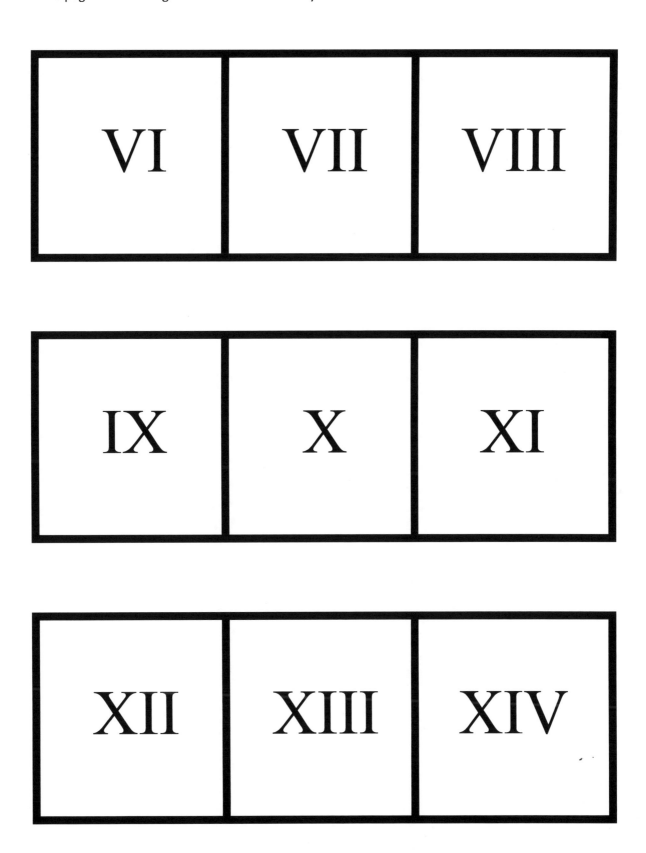

*This page is for cutting. The back is intentionally left blank.

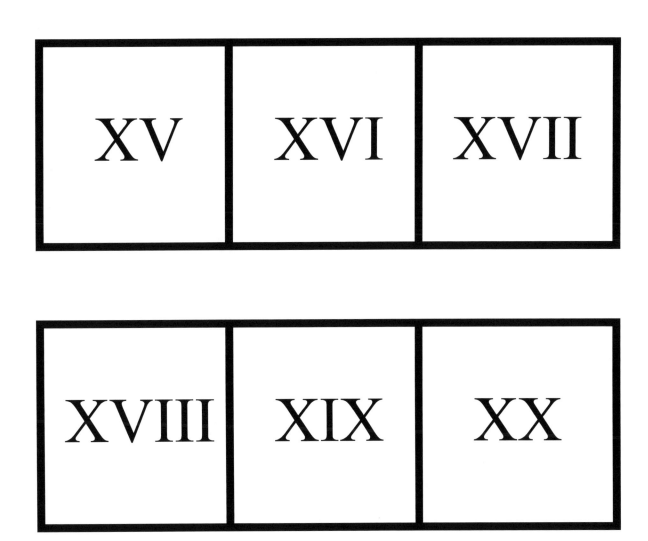

*This page is for cutting. The back is intentionally left blank.

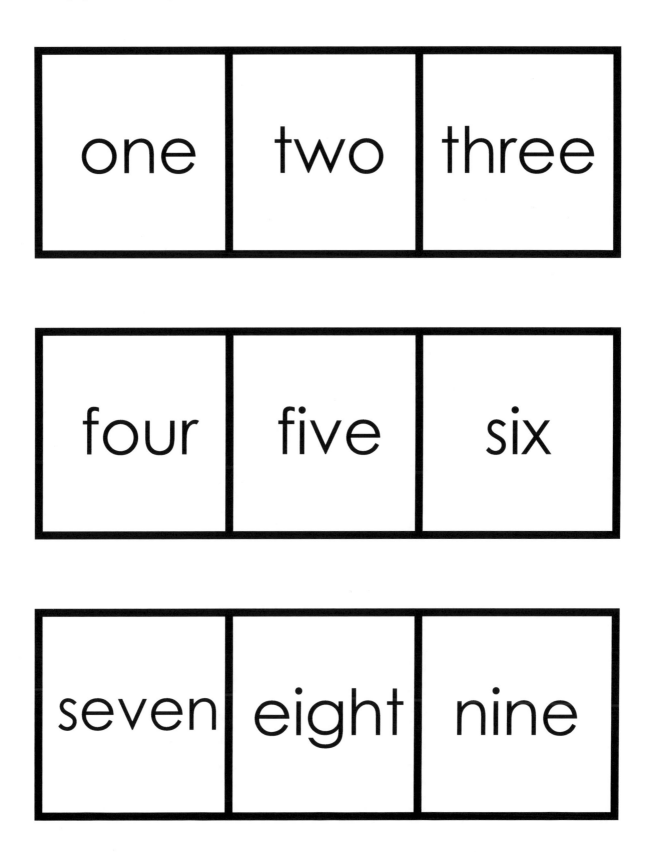

*This page is for cutting. The back is intentionally left blank.

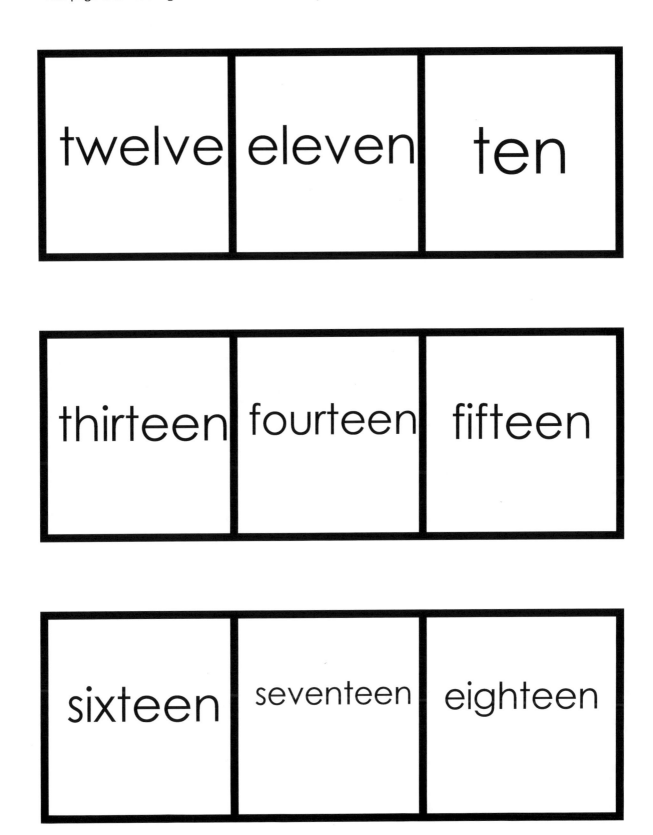

*This page is for cutting. The back is intentionally left blank.

| 1 | 2 | 3 |

| 4 | 5 | 6 |

| 7 | 8 | 9 |

*This page is for cutting. The back is intentionally left blank.

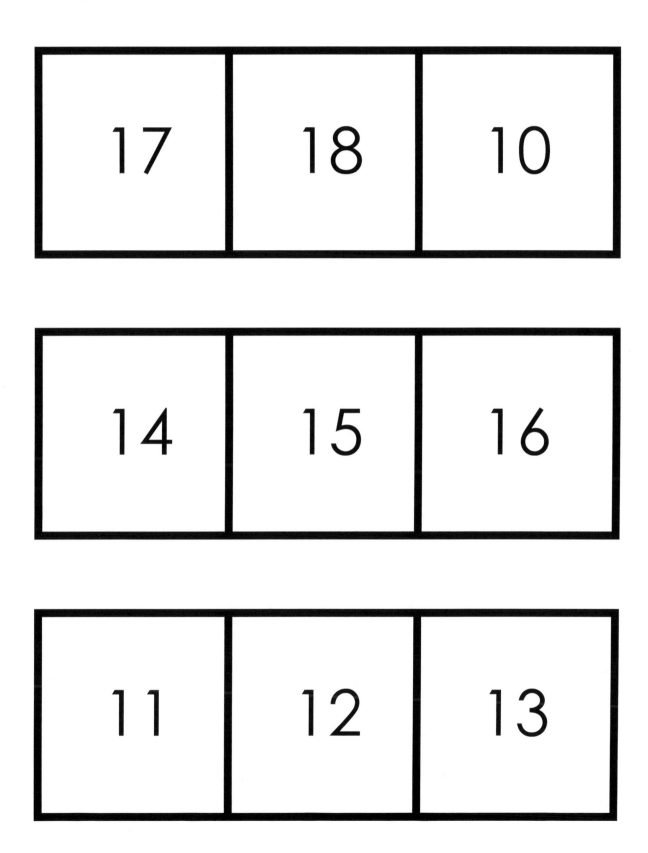

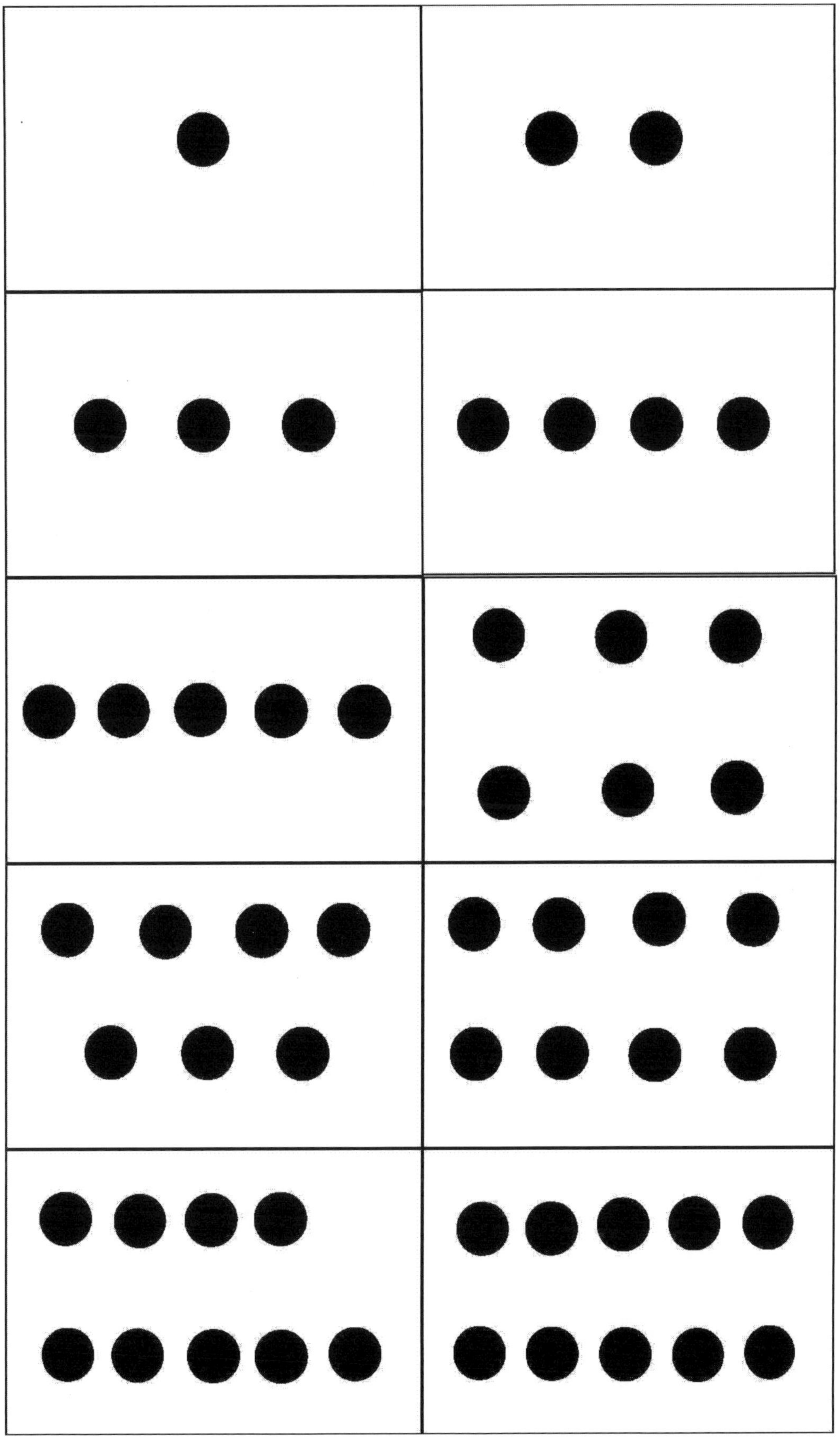

My Counting Book

My Name

How many animals do you see?

How many animals do you see?

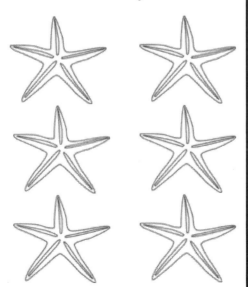

How many animals do you see?

How many animals

do you see?

How many animals

do you see?

How many animals

do you see?

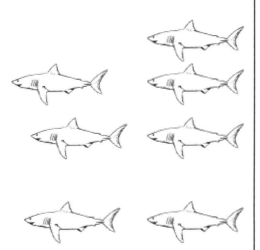

How many animals

do you see?

Sixty 60	Fifty 50
Seventy 70	Forty 40
Eighty 80	Thirty 30
Ninety 90	Cut it out in one big rectangle. Fold in half longways. Then fold it in half between the 70 and 80 and the 30 and 40. Then snip along the middle to separate the 70 from the 40 and the 80 from the 30. The 30 and 40 will be back to back. The 80 and 70 will be back to back. You can do that by pinching this and the 90 in one hand and the 50 and 60 in the other. Then bring your hands together.

Clothespin Counters

Fold this rectangle up behind the picture and words. Fold the two side flaps back and attach to this flap. You will have made a pocket. Then attach this to the lapbook. Inside go the dot cards.

Your child can take out each card and attach a clothespin to the dot. This is practicing one-to-one correspondence—in other words, counting.

5   10

15   20

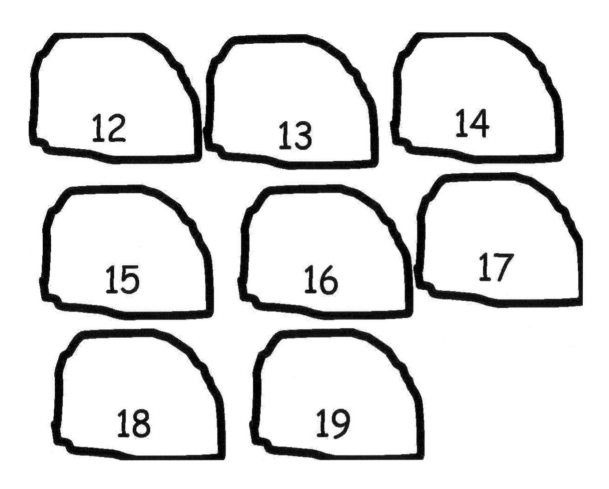

Cut out the ice cream cone with the 11 scoop. Cut out each number scoop and stack them — make a tall ice cream cone. (Or you could staple them in a stack) Color the ice cream scoops in different flavors.

| 10 | 9 | 8 | 7 | 6 |

| 5 | 4 | 3 | 2 | 1 | 0 |

Cut out the two strips. Use the little rectangle by the 5 to make it all one strip. Fold fan style so that the 10 is the cover. Use this piece to count backwards. The back of the 0 will attach to the lapbook.

20

0

21

1

22

2

23

3

24

4

25

5

Cut out each rectangle separately. Stack shortest to longest and staple along the top. You hopefully can see 0—9 along the bottom. I help my son know what number comes next by asking him what comes after 3 and then he can say 4 and then can figure out 24 is next. There is also room on most pieces for your child to write the number.

26

27

6

29

7

28

9

8

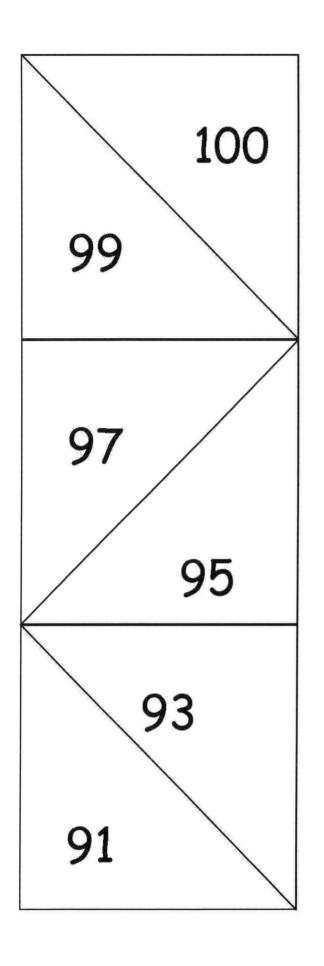

98

96

94

92

90

The back of 91 gets attached to the lapbook. Start at the 100 and fold along the lines into triangles. Keep folding on the lines, folding the triangle over and over itself. Write, or cut and glue, the even numbers to the backs of the triangles. 90 will go on the back of 93.

Made in the USA
Las Vegas, NV
05 September 2024